Sweet Dreams Yellowstone National Park

Adriane Doherty • Anastasiia Kuusk

Rubber Ducky Press
Carmel, IN

The sun rises as eager eyes open up to a new morning. We are going to explore Yellowstone National Park, searching for adventure.

Tall lodgepole pine trees stand in the rolling hills of the park. Nearby, a swallow feeds its young family. This is the perfect place to play hide and seek.

A baby porcupine is high up in the tree,
watching momma gather food to eat.
The squirrels are very fascinated with
what they see.

Don't get too
close. Ouch!

Yellowstone National Park is the perfect place to go hiking on the trails. Along the way is a family of deer, running and playing with each other. The yellow monkeyflowers are so beautiful in the summertime.

Hummingbirds flutter their wings around the colorful garden looking for pretty flowers to drink from.

The bison don't seem to mind all the visitors
that come to the park. Take the bike path
to Old Faithful and see the geyser spray
water into the sky. A rainbow forms, making
everything look so colorful!

On top of momma's back the youngest
baby cub feels very safe while watching
her brother and sister roll around and play.
They have so much energy!

The waterfall splashes down into the rocky bottom below. The gray wolf enjoys the mist that cools him down on a hot summer day.

The beavers are very busy preparing their home for the season. They are curiously watching as a family canoes across the water. Paddling Yellowstone's Shoshone Lake is always a fun adventure!

In the park, the badger and red fox are searching for food while the squirrels are running about gathering the acorns. They know fall is coming soon!

The icicles start to form on the entrance of the den. Momma grizzly bear and her baby lay sleeping for the winter.

Sweet dreams grizzly bears!

Friends gather around a roaring campfire toasting marshmallows and telling stories. Bedtime is drawing near.

Sweet dreams friends!

Old Faithful Inn is winding down for the night. The animals look so peaceful as they settle in.

Sweet dreams, dear little animals!

After a day of exploring, we are warm, cozy, and ready for a bedtime story.

Sweet dreams explorers!

Wow, what a busy day! I wonder what we will do tomorrow.

Sweet dreams Yellowstone National Park!

Sweet dreams everyone!

What did we see in Yellowstone National Park today?

Adriane Doherty is the author of 15 children's books. Her writing encourages curious young minds to learn about the people and places around them while sharing an entertaining story. Adriane attended college in Indiana. Following her schooling, she went into sales and currently works in finance and operations at a distribution company she co-founded with her husband. As the mother of three, Adriane read to her young children daily, and her love of books and helping young minds grow and understand the places around them inspired her to write.

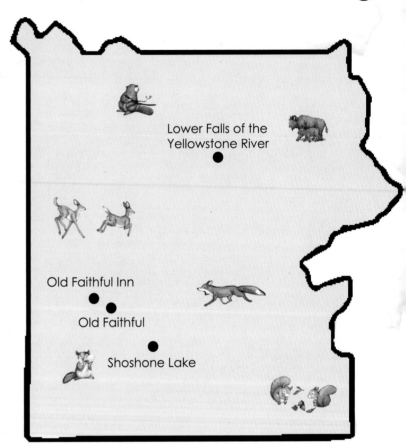

Lower Falls of the Yellowstone River

Old Faithful Inn

Old Faithful

Shoshone Lake

Other Rubber Ducky Press Titles You May Enjoy
ABC Down on the Farm • ABC Yellowstone • Wake Up, Woods • ABC Christmas • One Tomato
Purple Carrot • Chicken and Moodles • Worm & Bird Become Friends

Follow us on Instagram
@rubberduckypress

Find coloring pages at
rubberduckypress.com